SOLID
FOUNDATION
The Power of Praying Scripture

COMPILED BY
PRAYER CONNECT

PRAYERSHOP
PUBLISHING

Terre Haute, Indiana

This product represents the theme section of Issue 3 of *Prayer Connect* magazine. Because the message of this theme is so crucial to a believer's prayer life, we offer it in this smaller, booklet format as a way for churches to put it inexpensively in the hands of their people. Go to *prayershop.org* to see multiple copy discounts that are available.

PrayerShop Publishing is the publishing arm of Harvest Prayer Ministries and the Church Prayer Leaders Network. Harvest Prayer Ministries exists to equip the local church to become a house of prayer for all nations, releasing God's power for revival and finishing the task of world evangelization. Its online prayer store, *prayershop.org*, has more than 600 prayer resources available for purchase.

ISBN: 978-1-935012-30-6

3 4 5 6 7 8 9 10 11 12 | 2019 2018 2017 2016

The Bible on the cover belonged to prayer mentor, Evelyn Christenson, who went to be with the Lord in November 2011. The photo was taken by her son, Kurt Christenson. evelynchristensonministries.org .

CONTENTS

INTRODUCTION

Decades ago, she prayed a very bold prayer. Evelyn Christenson asked the Lord to let her teach the world to pray. She had a moment of thinking perhaps the prayer was not right, but then the Lord confirmed that *He* was the One who put that prayer on her heart.

When Evelyn passed away in November 2011 at age 89, it was clear that God had granted her request. She was the author of several best-selling books on prayer, she traveled internationally to teach principles of prayer, and even today her material is broadcast by radio into various countries of the earth.

God granted me the privilege of sitting under Evelyn's mentorship for the last few years. Not only did I experience her passion for prayer, but I also heard often of her love for God's Word. The two were inseparable. All of Evelyn's deep and impassioned prayer life flowed out of the rich truths she discovered daily in Scripture. As you can see by her Bible, pictured on our cover, Evelyn treasured the Word and let it saturate her life. She understood the power of praying God's Word.

My Own Journey

A few years ago the Lord convicted me about how much I *did not* know of His Word. My prayer life was rooted in my own thoughts and desires, but rarely did it flow out of my interaction with Scripture.

However, during an intense season of prayer, God impressed upon me to turn to His Word in a dramatic way. I unplugged the distraction of my television, and for the next several weeks I learned to pray Scripture. I started in Genesis and began praying my way through the Bible. God spoke to me and profoundly changed my heart. I fell in love with Jesus as He revealed Himself to me through His Word.

God answered my prayers in an amazing way during that season. But even after God had captured my heart, I continued praying through the

Bible, book after book. Daily I read passages and then prayed back to Him the truths I discovered.

As I prayed through the Old Testament, I began embracing repentance, obedience, holiness, and fear of the Lord. When I embarked on the New Testament, my longing for the manifest presence of Jesus Christ through revival and spiritual awakening started consuming my prayers. After three years, I finally prayed the ultimate invitation, "Come, Lord Jesus," at the end of Revelation.

Saturated in the Word

Both Evelyn and I discovered a foundational truth to prayer. When on your knees in prayer, keep God's Word in one hand as you extend the other hand in worship of God and His great mercies.

In this booklet, many faithful pray-ers and students of Scripture will share their experiences of the power and authority of prayer grounded in God's promises. May you discover the joy of saturating your prayer life with the Lord Himself as revealed by the Holy Spirit through His rich and treasured Word.

—Carol Madison, editor, *Prayer Connect*

By Dana Olson

The SCRIPTURE PRESCRIPTION

Overcoming Arrested Prayer Development

Todd felt helpless. He sat in his tiny apartment, staring through the dirty window at the partly cloudy day outside. The call had taken him by surprise.

"Son, there's no reason for you to be shook up by this—you've got so much to do with your youth work and studies—but Mom has a lump on her breast, and we thought you should know. Her appointment to get it checked out is next week. Your sister's nearby, so you don't need to feel like you have to come. Wait until we know more."

His dad's voice sounded the same as always, but with those last words, out came a deep sob. "Please, Todd, just pray for us. Please pray. You know how to pray."

Todd hadn't moved from his chair in the hour since the call, hadn't cried either. *This must be what shock feels like,* he thought. His mother . . . cancer . . . his dad's rare emotion . . . what must his sister be feeling? The stream of thoughts repeated in his mind, but what haunted him most were his father's words: "You know how to pray."

Suddenly a very plain, unadorned thought hit Todd hard: *I don't know how to pray.* Though all alone, Todd blushed red with the realization. It embarrassed him. He was a seminary student, youth worker at a small church, graduate of a well-known Christian university, raised in a good church by committed Christian parents, yet he was *at a loss to know how to pray!*

A Case of APD

Todd steered his old red pickup through the traffic and across the city to his old university. He searched high and low, finally discovering a lone parking spot in a packed lot. An odd mix of emotions hit him as he passed through the doorway and into the halls: familiarity and weirdness, home and "you don't belong here anymore." He knew right where to go, past the philosophy department office and into the Bible department hallway. He knocked gently, and a familiar voice responded, "Come in."

"Dr. Warren, thanks for taking time. So good to see you."

"Todd, I'm delighted you called." They shook hands firmly, then Todd sat in the ancient upholstered chair, where hundreds of students had sat before him. Todd spent many hours as a student in that chair, exploring the mind of his favorite professor, getting advice and perspective. That's what Todd needed now.

The two caught up quickly. Then Dr. Warren shifted the conversation. "Now, tell me why you've come."

It didn't take long for the former student to lay the circumstances before "the good Doctor" as Todd often called him. Before he was done, he found himself overcome with emotion, his head in his hands.

"Here's the hard truth, Doc. I don't know how to pray. I mean, I pray every day, several times a day. But really, beyond 'God bless the food and thanks and please give us a great youth night,' I don't know *how to pray.*" Todd said the last three words slowly, deliberately, even harshly.

He looked up now to the pondering Dr. Warren. "I understand completely. I've been where you are," he said. "Believe me, one can write books on theology and Bible commentaries and scholarly articles—and still not have the foggiest notion how to pray."

"But Doc, you *do* know how to pray. You prayed with us in class, here in your office, even in the hallway! You are one of the godliest men I know. Something must have changed."

"It did. And I'm going to tell you what it was. You have a very common condition, rampant in the church. I once had it. It's called APD."

Dr. Warren smiled, then turned serious. "Arrested Prayer Development. APD. Arrested development is the termination or interruption of a normal development process.[1] It's common in many disciplines, such as psychology, physical therapy, and speech. Arrested *Prayer* Development is the termination or interruption of a healthy, growing prayer life."

"Yes, that's me all right," Todd admitted. "But what do I do about it?"

"It's very simple, Todd. I won't even charge you for it," Dr. Warren said playfully. "You need the Scripture Prescription."

Todd had a small notebook with him and he wrote the words down as Dr. Warren said them.

> *The Bible is God's prescription for APD. The way to break through in your prayer life is to pray Scripture. Read Ephesians 6:17-18. Take the sword of the Spirit, the Word of God, praying in the Spirit. What God has brought together we ought not separate—the Bible and prayer. Pray the Bible!*

"Church history is full of examples of great people of faith whose lives were revolutionized when they began the discipline of praying the Bible," Dr. Warren continued. "Martin Luther. George Müller. Hudson Taylor. Taylor's children would wake up in the night and find him reading the Bible and praying by candlelight. Müller said he struggled to keep his mind on prayer until he learned to pray with his Bible open. He would read, then pray, read, then pray. Müller realized that letting the Bible set the agenda led into all kinds of prayer, such as exaltation, confession of sin, making various requests, thanking God, and the like."

Dr. Warren's office was now a classroom. "Understand, Todd: *This is what changed my prayer life.* I was where you are now for a long time. I felt stuck in a giant rut. 'God bless the missionaries. God bless my family. God help me. Thanks for the food.'

"Then, from reading about Christians of the past, and their prayer lives, and also reflecting on my study of the Bible, there it was. So obvious, I had to try it. Soon I was praying with God's Kingdom agenda in mind! I was praying God's will as God gave it to me. More than that—as I prayed Scripture

I was getting to know God personally. He spoke to me through His Word as never before! The Scripture Prescription is the way to overcome Arrested Prayer Development."

Todd looked up from his notes to see Dr. Warren's eyes almost dancing. He couldn't help smiling. "Tell me what to do."

As the teacher spoke, his student continued to scratch the words onto the page.

- *Don't make this complicated! Keep it simple. NOT reciting memorized portions (the Lord's Prayer).*
- *Choose a book of the Bible.*
- *Read a few verses each day (a paragraph or literary unit).*
- *Reflect on what you've read, jotting a few notes as thoughts come to mind.*
- *Ask, "Lord, how should I pray?"*
- *Read the verses again, slowly, chew on them.*
- *Then PRAY!*

"As you do this, Todd, it may seem awkward at first. It was for me. But, I can't stress this enough, keep on doing it! Don't stop. Make it a daily habit. A few verses a day, read-reflect-pray. And like taking a medication day after day, over time a whole new world of prayer will open up to you. You will be amazed."

A Greater Kingdom Agenda

Todd reviewed his notes early the next morning, sitting at his simple kitchen table. He fondly thought of Dr. Warren's big bear hug when Todd left the office. "God will heal your mother, Todd, on earth here, or in glory forever. Either way, I am excited for you because you're going to learn to pray in a way that can transform your life, and all those you influence, for years to come."

Todd had already been reading in 1 John, so that's where he turned. But instead of reading for a few minutes and then praying briefly for the day as he normally did, today he tried Dr. Warren's method. Here is what he wrote down in the notebook for that day:

- *1 John 3:16-18*
- *Jesus is our great example of love.*

- *What does it mean to "lay down our lives for the brothers"?*
- *Pray for persecuted Christians who are laying down their lives today for Christ.*
- *Help me be generous with others—don't let me "walk on by."*
- *Why are we tempted to talk about love but not really live that way?*

He read the passage twice, reviewed the notes he had jotted, reflected for a few moments, and then prayed. After praying through these thoughts, a couple specific examples came to mind of people he really needed God's help to love. He prayed for them by name. Then he prayed for his mother's health, his dad and sister, and a few other items he kept on a list.

Afterward, Todd had a clear realization: With his old way of praying, he would not have prayed about loving the difficult people in his life. He would not have prayed for persecuted Christians, and he probably wouldn't have thanked God that Jesus laid down His life for him. Praying the Bible had pushed him to pray with a greater Kingdom agenda, to pray specifics he wouldn't have thought of otherwise.

It was a start for Todd. Day after day he continued. Some days the praying came quickly and easily. Other days it felt painful! But Todd didn't stop. First, 2 and 3 John, then Ezra and Nehemiah in the Old Testament, then back to Jude and Revelation. Todd prayed through them all.

Prayer for Real

"Todd, thanks for your call. How's your mother doing?"

"Thanks for asking. She had surgery, and is doing fairly well. There is follow-up treatment. I spent Christmas there, and it was a special time for our family."

"And how's your prayer life, my friend?"

"Doc, that's why I called. I can't thank you enough. It's awesome. Praying God's Word has completely changed my prayer life. It's been several months now, and I'm sure I've got a lot more to learn, but wow, I can pray for an hour and not even think about it. And when I'm praying with others in my small group— or with our church staff, or the youth— consistently things I've been praying in the Bible will come out of me. Our pastor even said, 'Todd, you pray with such insight and depth, please tell us about it.'

"As a result, I got to teach the Scripture Prescription to our staff. I'm teaching our youth council leaders, too! Doc, I'm not saying it's perfection every day. But you were so right. Over time my prayer life has gotten healthier and my walk with God deeper. My walk with God is so much more intimate, and personal, and *real!*"

Todd could hear Dr. Warren's smile in his voice: "Whatever you do, don't stopping battling APD. This prescription has changed you, and it can change your youth group, and your church. Thanks be to God!"

[1]Thanks to Dr. Ned Stringham for his explanation of arrested development, many years ago. Also, seed ideas for this method of praying Scripture were discovered long ago in the powerful sermon, "The Power That Wields the Weapon," by Dr. John Piper.

. . . .

DANA OLSON is senior pastor of Faith Baptist Fellowship, Sioux Falls, SD. He directed Prayer First, the prayer mobilization ministry of Converge Worldwide (BGC), for 13 years. He is chairman emeritus of the Denominational Prayer Leaders Network. This story is a compilation of prayer experiences. Dana's use of the name Dr. Warren is a tribute to his friend and mentor Dr. Warren Wiersbe.

By Cheri Fuller

Blessing, Power, & Grace

Inviting into Our Lives Everything that God Has Ever Planned

S t. Augustine once blamed himself for all the lost time trying to find God's will when, from the very beginning, he could have found it by praying the Word.

Throughout our years of marriage, my husband and I have found that praying biblical prayers is a way to invite God's blessing, power, and grace into our lives. Many years ago, in our 20s, when we recommitted our lives to Christ and began a daily walk in His Word, I began praying biblical prayers for our marriage, for my husband Holmes, and for our three children.

Daily as I would read the Bible, I'd notice a special verse and I'd put a date by it—"For Holmes 5/88" or "For our marriage, 10/95." Then I'd write the verse on my current index prayer card or in a journal and pray it, often many times.

One of the first passages God led me to—as if He took a big highlighter and said, "This is what I want for Holmes"—was Psalm 1. So I wrote his name by it, and over the years I have prayed it scores of times for him: "Lord, may Holmes be a man who delights in your Word and meditates on it day and night—so he will be like a tree planted along the riverbank, bearing fruit in every season of his life. May his leaves never wither, and may he prosper in all he does" (see vs. 1-3).

A few years later, in a search at the library to find the meaning of his name, I discovered *Holmes* means "from the river" or "with roots going into the river." I didn't know this at the time I began praying Psalm 1, but God knew my husband was going to go through very trying times in his business life—and He wanted his roots to sink deep into the soil of Christ's love, feed on the truth of Scripture, and drink from the River of Life. When Holmes later suffered through several years of serious depression and seasons of financial drought as a builder, I continued to pray these verses for him. I've seen the fruits of those prayers and God's faithfulness.

God Knows Our Children

God can show us how to target our children's needs with just the right Scripture, even when they live away—on campus or across the world. I had prayed and prayed for our college son Chris (second oldest), but needed new direction from the Lord. So I asked Him to reveal a special verse that would be right in line with His heart toward our son.

One night soon after, I had a dream. In it, Chris was standing beside me, holding a Bible and pointing out a verse as if to say, "That's me, Mom." The verse was Acts 17:28: "For in him we live and move and have our being." I sensed the Spirit saying that this is the truth about our son and I should pray that he would realize who he is in Christ. For many years since, I've prayed Acts 17:28 for Chris—when he was in medical school, serving in Iraq as a battalion surgeon saving Marines' lives, and as a father and husband in medical practice. As the Spirit continues to point me back to this verse, He reminds me to remember that He is the One who began a good work in Chris and He will complete it (Phil. 1:6)!

I've never run out of scriptural prayers to pray—especially when praying our three children through childhood and adolescence, college years, marriage, and now praying for their children. A verse I prayed continually during my seven-year journey of prayer for our oldest son was Ephesians 1:17-18: *Lord, open the eyes of his heart and give him spiritual wisdom and understanding so he will grow in the knowledge of You. I pray that his heart will be flooded with light so he can understand the wonderful future You have for him.*

Justin did not appear to be walking in the light at the time nor did he seem spiritually inclined. In fact, he was enamored with the world and all it had to offer from high school through his first two years of college. As I continued praying Ephesians 1:17-18 and other verses for him, I gathered other mothers, concerned about their teens, to pray in agreement together each week. When my spirits flagged, God seemed to say, "Persevere in prayer and trust Me."

Then one summer day after his sophomore year at University of Oklahoma, when I was driving him across the city to get his overheated car stuck on the highway, he turned to me and said, "You know, Mom, I've been feeling so empty and lonely, being so far from God and trying to do everything on my own. I know that God hasn't moved; I have. But what I want more than anything is to have an intimate relationship with Christ, to really know Him."

Justin has never looked back and has been following the Lord ever since. Watching this devoted husband and father of two, who now also prays God's Word for his own children, I have been constantly encouraged by the Lord's faithfulness and grace in Justin's life and family.

As I discovered more of the treasures of God's Word and promises, one of my favorite prayers is based in 1 Peter 5:7: "Lord, thank You for inviting me to cast all of my cares upon You! Here's what I am burdened and worried about today . . . ." And then I roll my concerns, workload, and anxieties upon the Lord. Praying this verse on countless days has brought more peace into my heart than anything else I can think of—and certainly more than any stress relief the world might offer.

Breathing the Life of Jesus

In his book *Pierced by the Word,* John Piper said that our general prayers "become powerful when they are filled up with concrete, radical *biblical goals* for the people we are praying for."

We just celebrated 42 years of marriage and can look back on praying hundreds and hundreds of biblical prayers, not only for ourselves and our children, but also for friends, family, and sisters and brothers in Christ that we've had the opportunity to pray for in healing services, conferences in other countries and in our own community. Each time,

I've been filled with faith and hope, in the best of times and the worst of times.

Praying God's Word transformed my spiritual life and did something else: It got my focus off the problems or situations and onto the One who could help us, transform us, and—when needed—restore us. I knew praying Scripture wasn't an overnight quick fix, but my confidence in the Lord increased as I grew to trust Him to fulfill His promises in His way and time. And I was assured—even when the answers were long in coming—that He who said He is able to keep safe what we entrust to Him will do more than we can ask, think, or imagine, because of His riches in glory in Christ Jesus (Eph. 3:20-21).

You, too, can find the blessing of praying God's Word for your family and personal life. When we pray God's words and then love those around us through prayer, we breathe life—the life of Jesus, the living Word—into them and into our hearts. Who among us doesn't need more of Christ in our lives and His blessing in our family?

It Takes a Little Practice

While it may not come naturally for you to pray biblical prayers, it takes only a little practice to become comfortable with using God's Word as a powerful prayer prompt. For instance:

- Take the verse in which Jesus said, "I am leaving you with a gift—peace of mind and heart. And the peace I give is a gift the world cannot give. So don't be troubled or afraid" (John 14:27, NLT). Then pray it back to God in your own words and from the sincerity of your heart. For example, "Thank You, Jesus, for Your matchless gift of peace. I receive Your peace in my mind and in my heart so I won't be troubled or afraid."

- When we pray for someone who is suffering or in need, the Bible is full of compassionate prayers. Recently I was struck by reading Psalm 79:8 when a friend had major surgery and I prayed it right back to God on her behalf: "Let your tenderhearted mercies quickly meet Janet's need, Lord." I sent that prayer to her via text message in the hospital, and she received it when she got out of the recovery room. That prayer for God's tenderhearted mercies echoes from my spirit whenever anyone I know is in the ER, in personal distress, or in physical pain.

- Pray God's attributes. A verse such as Psalm 46:1 assures us that God will be our "refuge and strength, a very present help in trouble" (NKJV). We can call upon God's very nature and character when we pray it back to Him: "Lord, You said You will be our refuge and strength, a very present help in trouble. I ask You to let me experience Your sustaining grace, strength, and power so that problems won't weigh me down."

His Word Upholds the Universe

How incredible it is that through Jesus' sacrifice on the cross, heaven's windows are opened and each of us is given access to Almighty God, who hung the stars and moon in the sky and upholds the entire universe by His very Word!

What a marvelous gift God has given us in the treasure of His Word to guide and shape our prayers. In it we can discover His will for our marriages, families, ministries, and all areas of our lives.

Even more, when we *pray* His Word, we are asking that all He's planned in heaven will come into our lives on earth!

....

CHERI FULLER is a popular speaker and award-winning author of more than 40 books, including *The One Year Book of Praying Through the Bible, When Mothers Pray,* and *A Busy Woman's Guide to Prayer.* As executive director of Redeeming the Family, Cheri has been a frequent guest on national radio and TV. Her passion is to encourage women and inspire people of all ages to impact their world through prayer (*cherifuller.com*).

By Kim Butts

9 Compelling Reasons to Pray the Word

Years ago, I was taught how to pray the Word of God—and it revolutionized my prayer life. It is the ultimate prayer manual written by God Himself. The Bible always makes His will clear to us through the written Word. Anything the Holy Spirit makes known to us will always be in agreement with God's revealed Word.

Praying the Word sets people free! Wouldn't you like to pray with complete confidence and assurance that the Lord God Almighty will hear and answer the Kingdom-advancing prayers that are on His heart?

Following are some reasons why praying Scripture can empower your prayer life individually and corporately. As you incorporate the Word into your prayers, you will pray with greater boldness and effectiveness because you will be interceding in God's "good, pleasing and perfect will" (Rom. 12:2).

Praying Scripture Is Powerful Because . . .

1. **It reveals God's will for His Kingdom:** What is on God's heart? We need to discover the will of God through His revealed Word and pray it for the sake of His Kingdom! Here are just a few things that are on the heart of God:

- He wants us to love one another (John 13:34-35).
- He wants all people to be saved and to come to a knowledge of the truth (1 Tim. 2:1-4).
- He wants us to pray for workers to be sent into His harvest field (Matt. 9:37-38).
- He wants unity in the Body of Christ (John 17:20-26).

2. **Praying the Word gives us confidence and power in our prayers:** When you pray Scripture, you can be confident that it is powerful! *"If you*

believe, you will receive whatever you ask for in prayer" (Matt. 21:22). It is much easier for me to believe in God's Word as I pray than to depend solely upon what is in my own heart, which can sometimes be selfish and not focused upon the plans and purposes of God.

3. **The Word of God gives us a beautiful, full, rich vocabulary of prayer:** Pray Psalm 145 back to the Lord. As you do, focus all of the words back on Him as a prayer of praise! Then, as you pray through this psalm and others, write down words and phrases that speak of God and His character. Doing so will help you learn ways to describe Him so that your prayers don't wither from repetition.

4. **The Word of God helps us to keep our prayer lives fresh and exciting:** *"For the Word of God is alive and active. Sharper than any double-edged sword, it penetrates even to dividing soul and spirit, joints and marrow; it judges the thoughts and attitudes of the heart"* (Heb. 4:12). Have you experienced dry seasons in your prayer life? Applying the vocabulary of Scripture to your prayer life will enliven it!

5. **His Word reminds us to stay focused upon Him in prayer:** *"But my eyes are fixed on you, sovereign LORD . . ."* (Ps. 141:8). In good times or bad, we need to have our eyes fixed and focused upon the Lord. Take everything to the Lord prayerfully, asking Him to take charge and work His will in every situation that arises. Be sure that prayer is always your first response, not your last resort.

6. **Praying the Word of God and hearing it prayed, builds our faith in God's ability to hear and answer:** *"Consequently, faith comes from hearing the message, and the message is heard through the word about Christ"* (Rom. 10:17). When we hear the Word of Christ, it builds our faith. When we pray the Word of Christ, it demonstrates our faith in what He will do.

7. **Praying the Word of God protects us from sin:** *"I have hidden your word in my heart that I might not sin against you"* (Ps. 119:11). We can use Scripture in our prayer lives if the Word is hidden in our hearts, reminding us of righteous living.

8. **Praying the Word boldly strengthens our witness to unbelievers:** *"For it is God's will* *that by doing good you should silence the ignorant talk of foolish people"* (1 Peter 2:15). As you begin to pray bold prayers from the Word of God and He begins to answer, those who doubt or are uncertain of who Jesus is, will have to take another look.

9. We should pray Scripture *so that* God is honored and glorified! *"All your works praise you, LORD; your faithful people extol you. They tell of the glory of your kingdom and speak of your might, so that all men may know of your mighty acts and the glorious splendor of your kingdom"* (Ps. 145:10-12, emphasis added). Whenever you pray Scripture, you bring glory and honor to the Father! The "so that" prayer makes every prayer a Kingdom prayer—a God-honoring prayer that touches the heart of the Father!

When you pray God's will for your life and the lives of others, be prepared to be yielded and obedient if He should ask *you* to be the answer to the prayers you pray!

. . . .

KIM BUTTS is the cofounder of Harvest Prayer Ministries (with her husband Dave) and the author of *The Praying Family: Creative Ways to Pray Together.* She and Dave are coauthors of *Revolution on Our Knees: 30 Days of Prayer for Neighbors and Nations* and *Pray Like the King: Lessons from the Prayers of Israel's Kings.* These books are available from *prayershop.org.*

BY JOHN T. MAEMPA

DECLARING PRAYER

The Formidable Force of Praying the Word Out Loud

Anyone who accepts Jesus Christ as Lord and Savior soon learns that the Christian life is not without opposition. Evil spiritual forces opposed to the work of Christ are active in our world. Constant opposition comes from an enemy who, though usually unseen, is very real.

Paul wrote in Ephesians 6:12, "Our struggle is not against flesh and blood, but against the rulers, against the authorities, against the powers of this dark world and against the spiritual forces of evil in the heavenly realms." These forces are pervasive and powerful, and must be taken seriously. We can be thankful, however, that God equips us with the ability to both protect ourselves from, and do battle against, the enemy of our soul.

Our principal weapon in the battle is the Word of God. Immediately following his alert to believers in Ephesians 6, Paul instructed his readers to "put on the full armor of God, so that when the day of evil comes, you may be able to stand your ground, and after you have done everything, to stand" (v. 13). Paul then described the pieces of armor to be worn—the belt of truth, the breastplate of righteousness, the footgear representing readiness for battle, the shield of faith, and the helmet of salvation.

Notably, each piece of armor is for defense or protection from the "flaming arrows of the evil one" (v. 16). Then Paul instructs his readers to take the "sword of the Spirit, which is the word of God" (v. 17)—the only weapon for offense in the Christian soldier's armament.

Without breaking stride, Paul adds in verse 18,

"And pray in the Spirit on all occasions with all kinds of prayers and requests." Clearly, there is a vital relationship in spiritual warfare between wielding the Word and praying Spirit-led prayers. Prayer, coupled with the Word, is a formidable force.

Declare Scripture with Power

Because God's Word is alive, dynamic, and powerful, as Hebrews 4:12 describes, we can wield it boldly in warfare prayer. While our enemies, Satan and his forces, cannot read our thoughts, they can hear our declarations in prayer. And while we do not pray *to* our enemies, we certainly can direct prayer *at* them, declaring the truths and promises of Scripture.

I am intrigued by war documentaries, particularly those that focus on the various kinds of weaponry used, especially during World War II. Among the most amazing displays of military power were the naval bombardments used to "soften" enemy beachheads. Positioned miles from shore, the great guns on the naval warships would hurl round after round of explosive projectiles, breaking down enemy fortifications and allowing foot soldiers to move onto the beachheads, press inland, and take territory for freedom.

In much the same way, strategic intercessory prayer, enhanced by praying Scripture, can be directed at the strongholds of the enemy in spiritual warfare. Just as David cried out, "May God arise, may his enemies be scattered; may his foes flee before him" (Ps. 68:1), we can openly and boldly declare God's Word when confronting the enemy. As we do so, the strongholds are broken.

But why declare Scripture audibly?

Declare Scripture by Voice

Declaring Scripture aloud sharpens our focus. For example, when I pray for my own healing or for the healing of others, I often declare the familiar words of 1 Peter 2:24: "By his wounds [stripes] you have been healed." When praying for provision, I declare Matthew 6:33: "Seek first his kingdom and his righteousness, and all these things will be given to you as well."

Praying Scripture aligns our prayers with God's Word. As we pray God's promises and truths back to Him, He is pleased to respond with His grace and favor. Of course, we must be careful that we pray Scripture *to* God and not *at* Him, expecting Him to answer simply because we have used His Word in our prayer. God will not be manipulated. However, when we declare His Word in sincerity, He is pleased to answer.

Declaring Scripture audibly in prayer also helps to confirm God's Word in our hearts and minds and strengthens our trust in His promises. Beth Moore, in her book, *Praying Scripture: Breaking Free from Spiritual Strongholds*, relates this personal perspective: "In praying Scripture, I not only find myself in intimate communication with God, but my mind is being retrained, or renewed (Rom. 12:2), to think *His* thoughts about my situation rather than mine" (p. 8).

Indeed, as we pray God's thoughts, we are greatly strengthened and encouraged despite the circumstances we face.

Praying Scripture aloud is much more than just whistling in the dark when we're afraid or in difficult circumstances. As we boldly declare God's

Word in sincerity and truth, God releases power that provides deliverance, victory, and freedom in the spiritual realms. There is tremendous power in God's Word; there is tremendous power in prayer. When combined, there is nothing Satan and his forces can do to destroy us.

Apply the Searchlight

As noted earlier, Hebrews 4:12 describes the Word of God as "alive and active," and "sharper than any double-edged sword." God's Holy Word is much more than words on paper; it is living and dynamic, and able to reveal what lurks at the core of our being. The writer adds that the Word "judges the thoughts and attitudes of the heart. Nothing in all creation is hidden from God's sight. Everything is uncovered and laid bare before the eyes of him to whom we must give account."

In order for our prayers to be effective, we must regularly apply the searchlight of God's Word to our own lives. We must pray as did David, "Search me, God, and know my heart; test me and know my anxious thoughts. See if there is any offensive way in me, and lead me in the way everlasting" (Ps. 139:23). As we pray God's Word in our times of communion with Him, the Holy Spirit will direct His piercing light to reveal things that displease God and hinder our relationship with Him. Much of the time our thought life is where the greatest problem lies.

Our mind is a battleground on which the enemy easily prevails if we do not fill our thoughts with God's Word. While many thoughts we entertain originate with us, the enemy is also able to inject thoughts that are impure, untrue, and unholy. Paul instructed in 2 Corinthians 10:5 that victory in our spiritual battle is achieved when we "demolish arguments and every pretension that sets itself up against the knowledge of God, and we take captive every thought to make it obedient to Christ." Taking those thoughts captive requires intentional effort on our part as we counter Satan's attacks. We can successfully resist and reject unwholesome thoughts as we focus upon Jesus Christ and His Word and fill our minds with things that are true, noble, right, pure, lovely, admirable, excellent, and praiseworthy (Phil. 4:8).

Fill the Arsenal

In view of this, it is important that we commit Scripture to memory. Then, in those times of testing which sometimes come when we do not have access to a printed copy of God's Word, the Holy Spirit can help bring to our mind what we have stored in memory and do effective, victorious battle against the enemy. In so doing, we follow Jesus' example when He encountered Satan in the Wilderness Temptation (Matt. 4:1-11). As each temptation was placed before Him, Jesus responded with Scripture. The end result was that "the devil left him, and angels came and attended him" (vs. 11).

Here are some Scriptures put to prayer that pertain to specific issues or circumstances we might face. Fill your spiritual arsenal with these and other passages. Experience the power of wielding both the sword of the Spirit and prayer.

Anxiety or Worry

Thank You, oh God, for inviting me to cast my cares and burdens upon You. Thank You for sustaining me by Your great power. Please help me to stand and not fall in this time of worry and care (Ps. 55:22).

Help me, oh God, to be anxious about nothing. In the face of this test and trial, I bring my request for help to You with a thankful heart. Thank You for the awesome peace You give me even when it doesn't make sense to be at peace (Phil. 4:6-7).

Guidance and Wisdom

Father God, I thank You for ordering my steps and guiding me in the way I should take. I look to You again today for Your guidance and direction (Ps. 37:23).

Oh God, I really need wisdom today to make a right decision. You promise that if I lack wisdom, I can ask of You and You will give it generously—realizing I don't always know what to do. Please grant me Your wisdom today. Thank You for the marvelous help You provide (James 1:5).

Healing

I need Your healing touch today, oh God. Your Word declares that Your Son Jesus bore my sins on the cross so that I might receive Your salvation, and that Your wonderful gift of salvation includes the blessing of Your healing touch. Thank You for sending Your Son to die on the cross not only for my sins, but for my healing as well (1 Peter 2:24-25).

As I come to You in prayer for healing, oh God, I am so grateful that Your Word declares that the prayer offered in faith will make me well; that You will raise me up. I trust in that promise today (James 5:15).

Spiritual Warfare

Help me, oh God, to be self-controlled and on the alert for the enemy Satan who prowls around like a roaring lion seeking whom he can destroy. Help me resist him by standing firm in my faith just as many others have done (1 Peter 5:8-9).

In my walk with You, oh God, may I always be in submission to You and resist the devil. Help me to stay close to You and know the power and protection of Your presence day by day (James 4:7-8).

As you fill your spiritual arsenal with verses like these and many others, you will be well prepared to counter Satan's attack, demolish strongholds, receive help and healing, and live in victory. Remember, "The prayer of a righteous man [and woman] is powerful and effective" (James 5:16).

. . . .

JOHN T. MAEMPA is director of the Office of Prayer and Spiritual Care for the General Council of the Assemblies of God, Springfield, MO.

By Sandra Higley

PRAYING SCRIPTURE

This Bible study is formatted for small group open discussion. If you use this study by yourself, we suggest that you journal your answers to the discussion questions.

What's the Catch?

Matthew 21:22 tells us that if we believe, we will receive whatever we ask for in prayer. Yet how many times have we prayed—desperately and in earnest—only to experience disappointment? If prayer is an actual weapon of warfare with divine power (2 Cor. 10:3-5), why don't we see more answers?

The word for power in those verses is *dunatos* (our word *dynamite* comes from this root word).

Other places in the New Testament *dunatos* is translated *possible*: "With God all things are possible" (Matt. 19:26). God invites us repeatedly to partner with Him to do the impossible—so what's the catch?

The key to praying powder-keg prayers is simple: pray God's will. God is looking for men and women of radical faith who will ask for His will to be done on earth—right here, right now.

Discussion Questions

You can be bold and tenacious when you are praying God's will. Prayers in sync with His heart will not be denied. Based on 1 John 5:14-15, what gives us confidence as we approach God?

_____

_____

_____

_____

To pray God's will, you have to know God's will—and that's simple, too. He has already revealed Himself to us in His Word. *Praying Scripture is praying His heart.*

Obviously, we won't know, this side of heaven, how all of our prayers were answered. But generally speaking, do you think your current prayer life is effective? Why or why not?

_____

_____

_____

_____

_____

Describe your greatest struggles when it comes to prayer.

_____

_____

_____

_____

Cheri Fuller speaks of God's Word as the ultimate guide to shape our prayers because in Scripture we discover what He wants for every area of our lives. Praying God's Word means we give up our desires—our control—in exchange for His. Read

Isaiah 55:8-9 and discuss what giving up control feels like to you. Do you fear it?

Declaring Scripture aloud sharpens our focus, confirms God's Word to our hearts, and strengthens our trust, according to John Maempa. He says that the spoken Word releases power that provides deliverance, victory, and freedom. How do Proverbs 18:21a and Mark 11:23 confirm this?

In his article, Dana Olson talks about a common condition rampant in the church: *Arrested Prayer Development*. His prescription for this ailment consists of reading a few verses each day, reflecting on what you've read, and then asking the Lord how to pray, based on those verses. How might this method alter the way you pray now?

_____

_____

_____

_____

_____

Action Steps

Ready to give it a try?

Use the following Scriptures to shape prayers for your own life or for individuals the Lord brings to mind: Ephesians 1:17-19, 3:6-18; Colossians 1:9-10; 2 Thessalonians 2:16-17, 3:5; 2 Timothy 2:22-23; 1 Peter 1:22.

....

SANDRA HIGLEY is the author of several Scripture prayer guides in bookmark form, including *Prayers of Repentance, Partnering with God in the Struggle over Sin,* and *Life-Giving Prayers for Your Church.* You can order them from *prayershop.org.*